The Conflict Resolution Library™

Dealing with Teasing

• Lisa K. Adams •

The Rosen Publishing Group's
PowerKids Press™
New York

Published in 1997 by The Rosen Publishing Group, Inc.
29 East 21st Street, New York, NY 10010

First Edition

Book Design: Erin McKenna

Photo Credits: Cover and all photo illustrations by Seth Dinnerman.

Adams, Lisa K.
     Dealing with teasing / by Lisa K. Adams.
          p.   cm. — (The conflict resolution library)
     Includes index.
     Summary: Discusses why people tease, the difference between affectionate and mean or cruel teasing, and offers suggestions for how to deal with the latter.
     ISBN 0-8239-5070-0
     1. Teasing—Juvenile literature. [1. Teasing.]
     I. Title. II. Series.
BF637.T43A32 1997
303.6'9—dc21   97-4148
                                                                                      CIP
                                                                                      AC

Manufactured in the United States of America

Contents

Different Kinds of Teasing

People tease each other for many reasons. Some tease to show **affection** (uh-FEK-shun). A proud father might tell his daughter who loves to swim, "You're going to grow **scales** (SKAYLZ) if you spend too much time in the water!"

Some people tease to **communicate** (kuh-MYOON-ih-kayt). A girl might gently tease a shy classmate to get to know him better. But sometimes playful teasing can hurt.

◀ Some teasing can be friendly.

5

Knowing When to Stop

Playful teasing can be fun. But the fun only lasts as long as the teaser and the person being teased are both enjoying it.

When the person being teased stops having fun, then playful teasing can easily turn into **cruel** (KROOL) teasing. If you are teasing someone and he is not laughing or smiling anymore, you know that the teasing is no longer fun.

It's important to know when teasing stops being fun and starts being mean. ▶

Cruel Teasing

Cruel teasing can hurt people's feelings. Teasing can also affect people in other ways. A person who is teased may not want to go to school or play with friends anymore because he is afraid of being teased. Some kids are teased so badly they become angry. Sometimes they believe the awful things that others say about them. They may start to feel bad about themselves. Or they may try to hurt the person who is teasing them.

◀ Some teasing can get out of hand and turn violent.

You're Not Alone

Everyone gets teased in a mean way at one time or another. Students who get good grades are teased right along with those who don't get such good grades. Overweight children share the pain of being teased just as much as kids who are very thin. Tall kids get teased. So do short kids.

Kids are teased for all kinds of reasons. You may feel like you're the only one getting teased, but you aren't alone.

Even friends tease each other sometimes. ▶

Teasing As Protection

Some kids use teasing to make other people feel bad. Usually, the cruel teaser is **unsure** (un-SHER) of himself. Someone who teases you in a mean way usually doesn't feel very good about himself. He may want you to feel bad too. A teaser may not know whether other people like him or not. To protect himself, he will try to make others look bad.

◄ Teasing always says more about the teaser than about the one being teased.

It's Easy to Join In

Sometimes a nice person may tease others.
This person was probably teased in the past.
Being teased hurt her feelings so much that
she doesn't ever want it to happen again.
When she sees someone else being teased,
she is glad that she is not the **target** (TAR-get)
anymore. And to keep it that way, she may
join in with the teasing.

Often the teaser has nothing against you.
She may just be afraid for herself.

Someone may join in with teasing to ▶
protect herself from being teased.

Are You a Cruel Teaser?

Have you ever teased someone at school, knowing that it hurt his feelings? Many kids have done this at one time or another.

If you tease someone else, try to remember how you felt when you were teased. Do you want someone else to feel the same way you did? People who hurt others sometimes don't think about other peoples' feelings. Chances are, you don't want to be thought of that way.

◄ The next time you tease someone, think about how you felt when you were teased.

17

What to Do About Teasing

The best thing to do about someone who teases you is to **ignore** (ig-NOR) him. He wants to see you hurting so he can feel better about himself. Don't let him get what he wants. Show him that teasing does not bother you. Be yourself and don't listen to the silly things he says. Pretty soon, the teaser will leave you alone when he sees you are not letting him bother you.

Ignoring a person who teases you will show him that what he says doesn't hurt you. ▶

Teasing Hurts

Teasing hurts. Some people might tell you to ignore your feelings. But it's important to **recognize** (REK-ug-nyz) how you feel. If you are being teased, it's okay to be upset. You can cry about it if you want to.

You can also talk to someone about how you feel. Find an adult you trust. He or she can also help you talk about your feelings.

◀ It's okay to let your feelings out if you're upset.

You Are Special

You are an important person. Your family and friends know that. And you have things about you that are special.

You can handle teasing. The best way to battle teasing is to focus on the good parts of yourself. Realize that what a person who teases says is not true. If you feel good about yourself, what others say won't matter very much.

Glossary

affection (uh-FEK-shun) Friendliness or love toward someone or something.

communicate (kuh-MYOON-ih-kayt) Letting others know what you are feeling and thinking.

cruel (KROOL) Very mean.

ignore (ig-NOR) To pay no attention to.

recognize (REK-ug-nyz) Be aware of.

scales (SKAYLZ) Small, thin coverings on some fish.

target (TAR-get) A person or thing that is made fun of.

unsure (un-SHER) Not certain about something.

Index